I want to
this Book
I think people can get
a lot of interesting stuff.
People can learn a lot
of good stuff with this
book.

Raymundo
López

Research Scientist

CAREERS WITH CHARACTER

Careers with Character

Research Scientist

by Shirley Brinkerhoff

MASON CREST PUBLISHERS

Mason Crest Publishers Inc.
370 Reed Road
Broomall, Pennsylvania 19008
(866) MCP-BOOK (toll free)
www.masoncrest.com

First printing
1 2 3 4 5 6 7 8 9 10
Library of Congress Cataloging-in-Publication Data on file at the Library of Congress.
ISBN 1-59084-323-1
       1-59084-327-4 (series)

Design by Lori Holland.
Composition by Bytheway Publishing Services, Binghamton, New York.
Printed and bound in the Hashemite Kingdom of Jordan.

Photo Credits:
Corbis: pp. 78, 80, cover
Corel: pp. 16, 18, 48, 54, 58
PhotoDisc: pp. 4, 6, 7, 9, 10, 14, 20, 21, 24, 26, 27, 28, 30, 34, 36, 37, 38, 39, 42, 44,
    46, 52, 55, 56, 67, 70, 72, 73, 74, 75, 81, 82

Contents

We each leave a fingerprint on the world.
Our careers are the work we do in life.
Our characters are shaped by the choices
we make to do good.
When we combine careers with character,
we touch the world with power.

INTRODUCTION

by Dr. Cheryl Gholar
and Dr. Ernestine G. Riggs

In today's world, the awesome task of choosing or staying in a career has become more involved than one would ever have imagined in past decades. Whether the job market is robust or the demand for workers is sluggish, the need for top-performing employees with good character remains a priority on most employers' lists of "must have" or "must keep." When critical decisions are being made regarding a company or organization's growth or future, job performance and work ethic are often the determining factors as to who will remain employed and who will not.

How does one achieve success in one's career and in life? Victor Frankl, the Austrian psychologist, summarized the concept of success in the preface to his book *Man's Search for Meaning* as: "The unintended side-effect of one's personal dedication to a course greater than oneself." Achieving value by responding to life and careers from higher levels of knowing and being is a specific goal of teaching and learning in "Careers with Character." What constitutes success for us as individuals can be found deep within our belief system. Seeking, preparing, and attaining an excellent career that aligns with our personality is an outstanding goal. However, an excellent career augmented by exemplary character is a visible expression of the human need to bring meaning, purpose, and value to our work.

Career education informs us of employment opportunities, occupational outlooks, earnings, and preparation needed to perform certain

1

tasks. Character education provides insight into how a person of good character might choose to respond, initiate an action, or perform specific tasks in the presence of an ethical dilemma. "Careers with Character" combines the two and teaches students that careers are more than just jobs. Career development is incomplete without character development. What better way to explore careers and character than to make them a single package to be opened, examined, and reflected upon as a means of understanding the greater whole of who we are and what work can mean when one chooses to become an employee of character?

Character can be defined simply as "who you are even when no one else is around." Your character is revealed by your choices and actions. These bear your personal signature, validating the story of who you are. They are the fingerprints you leave behind on the people you meet and know; they are the ideas you bring into reality. Your choices tell the world what you truly believe.

Character, when viewed as a standard of excellence, reminds us to ask ourselves when choosing a career: "Why this particular career, for what purpose, and to what end?" The authors of "Careers with Character" knowledgeably and passionately, through their various vignettes, enable one to experience an inner journey that is both intellectual and moral. Students will find themselves, when confronting decisions in real life, more prepared, having had experiential learning opportunities through this series. The books, however, do not separate or negate the individual good from the academic skills or intellect needed to perform the required tasks that lead to productive career development and personal fulfillment.

Each book is replete with exemplary role models, practical strategies, instructional tools, and applications. In each volume, individuals of character work toward ethical leadership, learning how to respond appropriately to issues of not only right versus wrong, but issues of right versus right, understanding the possible benefits and consequences of their decisions. A wealth of examples is provided.

What is it about a career that moves our hearts and minds toward fulfilling a dream? It is our character. The truest approach to finding out who we are and what illuminates our lives is to look within. At the very heart of career development is good character. At the heart of good character is an individual who knows and loves the good, and seeks to share the good with others. By exploring careers and character together, we create internal and external environments that support and enhance each other, challenging students to lead conscious lives of personal quality and true richness every day.

Is there a difference between doing the right thing, and doing things right? Career questions ask, "What do you know about a specific career?" Character questions ask, "Now that you know about a specific career, what will you choose to do with what you know?" "How will you perform certain tasks and services for others, even when no one else is around?" "Will all individuals be given your best regardless of their socioeconomic background, physical condition, ethnicity, or religious beliefs?" Character questions often challenge the authenticity of what we say we believe and value in the workplace and in our personal lives.

Character and career questions together challenge us to pay attention to our lives and not fall asleep on the job. Career knowledge, self-knowledge, and ethical wisdom help us answer deeper questions about the meaning of work; they give us permission to transform our lives. Personal integrity is the price of admission.

The insight of one "ordinary" individual can make a difference in the world—if that one individual believes that character is an amazing gift to uncap knowledge and talents to empower the human community. Our world needs everyday heroes in the workplace—and "Careers with Character" challenges students to become those heroes.

Research scientists study the wonders of our universe.

1

JOB REQUIREMENTS

Knowing science can enrich your life.
Basically, science is a foundation
for genuine common sense.
—Lap-Chee Tsui, Canadian molecular
geneticist and winner of the Nobel Prize

For many of us, visiting the doctor to get a prescription for ***antibiotics*** is an ordinary experience. We expect medicines such as penicillin to quickly cure ear infections, strep throat, and other bacterial infections. But antibiotics—once considered miracle drugs—have only been available for just over half a century.

When Sir Alexander Fleming (1881–1955), a doctor and research bacteriologist at St. Mary's Hospital in London, served in World War I, he was deeply distressed by the high number of soldiers who died from bacterial infection of their wounds. After the war, Dr. Fleming decided to study bacteria. One day in 1928, he noticed mold growing in one of his laboratory cultures. Instead of throwing the contaminated culture away, he observed it carefully and saw that wherever the mold was growing, it appeared to have destroyed the bacteria. Because the mold was a species of *Penicillium*, he named it penicillin. He studied and experimented with the mold, and though it took many more years of research before penicillin was prescribed for people, the antibiotics we are so familiar with today resulted from his research.

Scientists have increased our understanding of weather patterns.

Sir Alexander Fleming, like other research scientists, had learned how to collect, organize, analyze, and interpret data. He used these tools in the discovery of penicillin, and his work has helped save millions of lives that would otherwise have been lost to bacterial infections.

Other diseases, such as poliomyelitis (polio), could not be stopped by antibiotics. Until the middle of the 20th century, polio was a dreaded illness that frequently crippled or paralyzed young people. Then Jonas Edward Salk (1914–1995), associate professor of bacteriology and head of the Virus Research Laboratory at the University of Pittsburgh School of Medicine, began research on a polio vaccine. It took several years to develop the vaccine and to conduct all the field tests necessary to prove that it was effective against all three viruses that caused polio, but by 1955 his research was done. Jonas Salk's vaccine was soon available throughout the United States and has nearly wiped out polio in developed countries everywhere.

Today, medical research scientists around the world continue to collect, organize, analyze, and interpret data as they work to develop new drugs and medical techniques to combat disease and make life better for future generations. Other researchers work in different areas, including environmental, earth, and social sciences.

This book will focus mainly on medical and biological research. Biological scientists who do biomedical research are called medical scientists. Most biological scientists and nearly all medical scientists work in the area of research and development. Often these medical scientists must combine their work as researchers, or as head of a research team composed of graduate and postdoctoral students, with teaching responsibilities at a university. Today, researchers frequently work alongside engineers, business managers, technicians, and scientists of other disciplines to develop new products. Those who do applied research and product development for private industry must understand the business impact of their work, which must be in line with the firm's products and goals, and may find they have less freedom to choose their own area of research. They may also have to work with nonscientists who have the power to veto or approve their ideas.

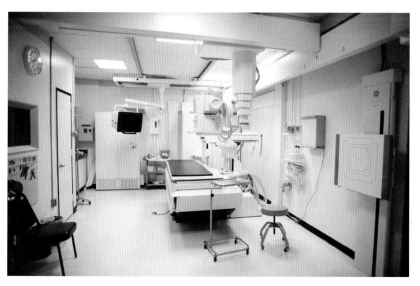

Our modern world of medicine was created and continues to be shaped by research scientists.

Researchers usually work regular hours in offices or in laboratories, where they often use electron microscopes, computers, thermal cyclers, and other equipment. Some experiments include the use of laboratory animals. If researchers work with dangerous organisms or toxic substances, strict safety procedures must be followed in order to avoid contamination. Some medical scientists work in hospitals or clinics, and administer drugs to patients in *clinical trials*. Many such scientists commonly depend on grant money to support their research and must conform to detailed grant-writing specifications when they prepare proposals for new or extended funding.

In the last few decades, rapid advances in knowledge related to genetics and molecules have opened new fields to research scientists. In 1954, Watson and Crick first described the structure of *DNA*. During the mid-1970s, two different methods of determining the order of the base pairs of the DNA sequence were announced. By 1978, scientists understood that, in order to be useful to the scientific community, vast amounts of information about DNA needed to be catalogued systemat-

In 1998, there were about 112,000 biological and medical scientists in the United States. Four out of ten biological scientists worked for either the federal, state, or local governments. Those employed by the federal government worked mainly for the U.S. Departments of Agriculture, the Interior, and Defense, or in the National Institutes of Health. The rest were employed in the drug industry, hospitals, or research and testing laboratories. Two out of ten worked in state government, and the rest worked in research and testing laboratories, educational institutions, the drug industry, and hospitals. Other biological and medical scientists held faculty positions in biology at colleges and universities.

Adapted from U.S. Department of Labor's *Occupational Outlook Handbook*, 2001.

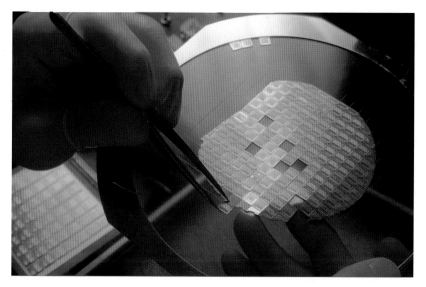

Research scientists may require manual dexterity to do their jobs well.

ically. Twin databases were established in Europe and the United States, just as personal computers began to prove their usefulness in biology laboratories. Out of the large organized effort to sequence and catalog this information came the ***Human Genome Project***, a coordinated effort by the Department of Energy and the National Institutes of Health. One goal of sequencing the ***genome*** is to use such research as a tool to understand the genetic origins of cancer and other life-threatening diseases.

Another area of research that is increasingly in the news is that of ***cloning***. In Scotland, on February 24, 1997, scientists announced the birth of a lamb named Dolly, cloned from a sheep's udder. Since then, experiments in cloning have been ongoing. In February 2002, scientists announced the birth of the world's first cloned domestic cat, called Cc in honor of the project that created her—Copy Cat.

These and other advances in biological research have been met

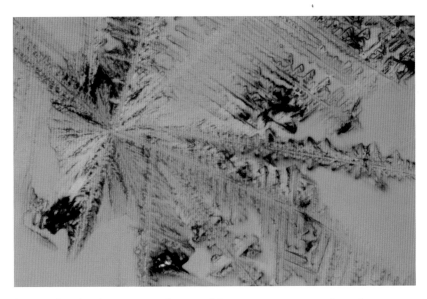

Research scientists may study something as enormous as the galaxy—or as tiny as ice crystals.

with a variety of responses, from enthusiastic reception to outright hostility. Researchers must increasingly examine the methods and motives of their work, and be able to explain and justify it.

Many colleges and universities offer the training needed to do biological research. Bachelor's degrees in biological science include courses in chemistry and biology, as well as mathematics and physics. Computer courses are also essential, because computers are now used for modeling and simulation tasks, the collection and organization of data, and statistical analysis. Graduates with a bachelor's degree are not usually able to work on their own projects in a laboratory setting. They are more likely to work as research assistants, biological technicians, medical laboratory technologists, or even, with additional courses in the field of education, high school biology teachers.

A master's degree qualifies biological scientists for some jobs in product development or in management, inspection, sales, and service. Advanced degree programs emphasize subfields such as microbiology or botany, and include fieldwork, laboratory research, and a thesis or dissertation, but such coursework may not be available at all colleges or universities.

Because the work of medical scientists is almost solely research oriented, a Ph.D. degree in a biological science is considered the minimum education required. This degree qualifies the scientist to research basic life processes and specific diseases or medical problems, and to analyze and interpret the results of experiments on patients. Those who administer drug or gene therapy to human patients, or who perform in-

Biological and medical scientists study living organisms and the ways in which these organisms relate to their environment. Biological scientists are also classified by the organism they study or by the activity they perform. Below are some of the different types of biologists:

Aquatic biologist: Study animals and plants that live in water.

Biochemists: Study the chemical composition of living things; analyze components of metabolism, reproduction, growth, and heredity.

Botanists: Study plants and their environment.

Marine biologists: Study organisms that live in salt water.

Microbiologists: Study microscopic organisms such as bacteria, algae, or fungi. Medical microbiologists focus on the relationship between organisms and disease, including the effects of antibiotics.

Physiologists: Study life functions of plants and animals, often specializing in areas such as growth, reproduction, photosynthesis, respiration, or movement.

Zoologists and wildlife biologists: Study animals and wildlife. Zoologists are further identified by the animal group they study: ornithologists (birds), mammalogists (mammals), herpetologists (reptiles), and ichthyologists (fish).

vasive procedures on patients, must also have a medical degree. It is common for medical scientists to spend several years in a postdoctoral position, gaining valuable experience in specific processes and techniques, before they apply for permanent jobs.

Academic qualifications are not the only essentials for successful work as a research scientist. Patience and objectivity are crucial, as is the ability to work either independently or as part of a team. Communicating clearly and concisely, both orally and in writing, is also essential. Because research scientists in the medical and biological fields deal with such important issues of life and death, it is vital that they be people of character. In the following chapters we will look at several core character qualities that are important for researchers, as well as for people in many other professions. These qualities include:

- integrity and trustworthiness
- respect and compassion
- justice and fairness
- responsibility
- courage
- self-discipline and diligence
- citizenship

As research scientists pursue their work within the context of these character qualities and abilities, they have the opportunity to make a meaningful contribution to our world. Because scientific knowledge is advancing so rapidly, scientists must also develop the ability to make ethical decisions. Choices must be made not only about our *ability* to do certain things (cloning, etc.), but also about the *advisability* of doing them. The following chapter will present some of the tools and procedures necessary for making difficult ethical decisions.

This is the true joy of life—being used for a purpose that is recognized by yourself as a mighty one.

—George Bernard Shaw

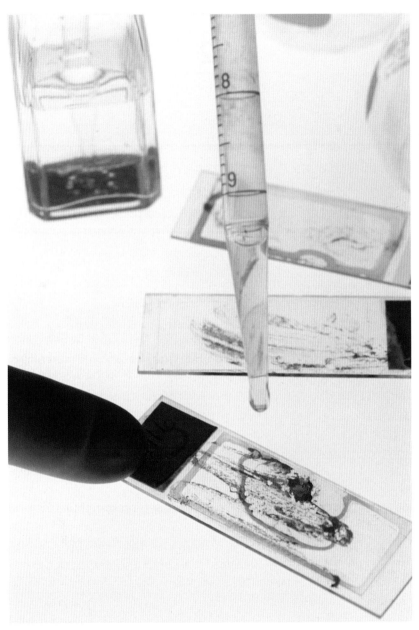

Because research scientists' work touches the lives of countless people, research scientists need to possess integrity and trustworthiness.

2

INTEGRITY AND TRUSTWORTHINESS

The trust of another person is a
treasure to be prized.

Sharon Entmann discovered that she had advanced breast cancer when she was only 38 years old. Her husband and three children were horrified at the thought that she might not survive. When Sharon and her husband were presented with treatment options, a research study done in South Africa showed strong evidence that women treated with high-dose chemotherapy delivered through bone-marrow transplants gave patients a much better chance of surviving advanced breast cancer. Sharon was disturbed to learn, however, that super-high doses of chemotherapy not only killed resistant cancer cells, but could also kill the patient by destroying his or her disease-fighting immune system.

Sharon desperately wanted to live to raise her children and share many more years with her husband. She agonized over the decision of which treatment she should choose. When she remembered what her doctor had told her about the research study done in South Africa, she wanted to sign up for a bone-marrow transplant right away. But when she thought about the possible side effects, she couldn't overcome her fear and dread of what might happen to her.

In the end, Sharon decided she couldn't go through with the bone-marrow transplant, even though she felt guilty about her decision. She called her *oncologist* and told him that she wanted only the standard *chemotherapy*.

A year later, while watching an evening television news program, Sharon and her husband were stunned to hear that the South African research study was now being questioned. The study, conducted by Werner Bezwoda of the University of Witwatersrand in Johannesburg, was the only one that had clearly demonstrated that bone-marrow transplants for breast cancer sufferers could prolong life, but the study's lead investigator was now accused of falsifying data.

Doctors from the United States had traveled to South Africa to check the data from Bezwoda's study, but could not find the records of several patients who had supposedly been involved in the study. The University of Witwatersrand began investigating Bezwoda for misrepresenting the results of his study, which is considered scientific miscon-

Research scientists are working to discover cures for deadly diseases like cancer.

> ### The Scientific Method
>
> Scientists usually use the following plan (or one very similar) when they conduct their experiments:
>
> 1. Identify a problem.
> 2. State a hypothesis (a statement explaining what is to be tested, the purpose of the investigation, and what the investigator hopes to prove or disprove).
> 3. State a procedure (a plan to help find a solution).
> 4. Perform the experiment, which means following the procedure stated in step number 3.
> 5. Record data (the factual information used as a basis for reasoning, discussion, or calculation).
> 6. Publish results so others may verify or repeat the experiment.

duct. Eventually, it was announced that Bezwoda's study had been "discredited."

The university released a statement in which Bezwoda was quoted as saying, "I acknowledge my error and take sole responsibility. This was done out of a foolish desire to make the presentation more acceptable. . . ."

Sharon and her husband knew that thousands of women with advanced breast cancer had undergone the pain and risks of a bone-marrow transplant, influenced at least in part by scientific research studies that indicated this course could help them live longer, healthier lives. Now, that information had been declared unreliable. Sharon felt a huge sense of relief that she had not subjected herself and her family to such a difficult experience. But she also felt sadness and anger on behalf of patients who had trusted the published research results and been misled.

Integrity and trustworthiness are critical in research scientists. One researcher's conduct in the laboratory and office has the potential to hurt and disillusion many, many people.

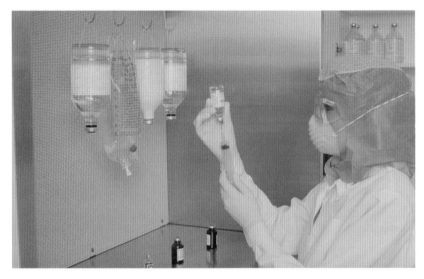

Human errors can easily be made while a scientist is doing research. Errors based on deception are far more serious.

Deception in Science

Scientists are humans, and so are prone to making honest errors, as well as errors caused by negligence. Far more serious are errors that involve deception. Such errors may involve:

- Fabrication (making up data or making up results)
- Falsification (misreporting or actually changing the data or results)
- Plagiarism (using another person's words or ideas without giving him or her credit)

The word "trustworthy" is easier to understand if you take the word apart and see that it means being worthy of, or living up to, another's trust or confidence. "Integrity" means firm adherence to a code of moral values; it comes from the word "integer," which means a whole, undivided number. When we say that people have integrity, we mean that, in their commitment to truth and moral values, they are the same through and through. Because of that, a person of integrity merits our trust. Because scientists do research on matters that affect all of us in one way or another, the public has the right to expect them to be honest and trustworthy—to be people of integrity.

Research scientists, however, can find themselves under pressure to report findings and make discoveries that are considered breakthroughs in their field. For research scientists, as for people in other professions, the desire to "get ahead" can be a major motivator. New discoveries can lead to recognition from peers and even from the public, and sometimes to a higher salary. Scientists must continually weigh the natural desire for advancement against the obligation to work for the good of others.

> **The four enemies of integrity:**
>
> - self-interest (The things we want . . . the things we might be tempted to lie, steal, or cheat to get.)
> - self-protection (The things we don't want . . . the things we'd lie, steal, or cheat to avoid.)
> - self-deception (When we refuse to see the situation clearly.)
> - self-righteousness (When we think we're always right . . . an end-justifies-the-means attitude.)
>
> Adapted from materials from the Josephson Institute of Ethics, 4640 Admiralty Way, Suite 1001, Marina del Rey, California 90292.

Questions such as whether or not to tell the truth about research data may seem like easy ones to answer. We have even *codified* what society thinks is moral or immoral on such questions, and research institutes have guidelines for ethical behavior. Inside the world of research, however, other more difficult decisions sometimes have to be made. Here are some examples:

- Ed was a research scientist who took a job working for a specific company. He had signed an agreement that his data would be kept confidential within that company. When he made a medical discovery he knew could help relieve the pain of thousands, perhaps millions, of people in severe pain, he wanted to publish his results immediately, in order to help as many people as quickly as possible. However, publishing his data would make his discovery available to researchers from competing companies, something he had promised not to do.

Three Foundations for Ethical Decision-Making

1. Take into account the interests and well-being of everyone concerned. (Don't do something that will help you if it will hurt another.)
2. When a character value like integrity and trustworthiness is at stake, always make the decision that will support that value. (For example, tell the truth even though it may cost you some embarrassment.)
3. Where two character values conflict (for instance, when telling the truth might hurt another person), choose the course of action that will lead to the greatest good for everyone concerned. Be sure to seek all possible alternatives, however; don't opt for dishonesty simply as the easiest and least painful way out of a difficult situation.

Adapted from materials from the Josephson Institute of Ethics, 4640 Admiralty Way, Suite 1001, Marina del Rey, California 90292.

Many research scientists do experiments on live animals. Some people feel this is cruel, while others believe that animal experimentation is justified by the benefits reaped from this research.

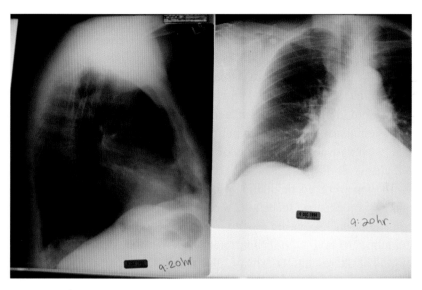

X rays and other medical technology would not exist today without the work of research scientists.

Ed's own company insisted he was obligated not to disclose his data until his employer could establish intellectual property rights to it. Ed knew he had an ethical obligation to his employer. He also knew that many people would suffer needlessly if his company held up the process too long.

- When Sheila, a post-doctoral researcher at a leading research hospital, was only months away from

A PERSON OF CHARACTER . . .

is trustworthy . . .
tells the truth.
does not mislead others.
does not steal or cheat.

has integrity . . .
shows commitment and courage.
stands up for his or her beliefs.
resists social pressures to do
   wrong.

Adapted from Character Counts Coalition, 4640 Admiralty Way, Suite 1001, Marina del Rey, California 90292.

publishing the results of a major study in which she'd been involved for over a decade, she was asked to review a paper by another researcher. While reading the paper, she discovered that the other scientist's research results contradicted her own in one area. Sheila was faced with the question of whether or not she should investigate these contradictory findings, a process that could set back her own publishing date significantly or perhaps even invalidate her years of work.

If you were Ed or Sheila, what steps would you take in order to make your decision? Questions such as these require much thought and consideration. Scientific institutions are working to establish clear guidelines to help with difficult decisions, but the personal values and morals of the researchers always play a significant part in the process.

Truth is the property of no individual but is the treasure of all.

—Ralph Waldo Emerson

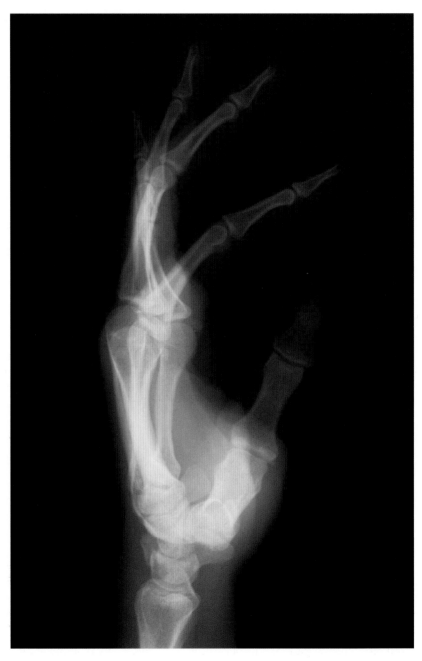

Leprosy causes the deterioration of patients' fingers and other extremities.

3

RESPECT AND COMPASSION

*When we combine our professional skills
with respect and compassion for
others, we can accomplish
great things.*

When Paul Brand was growing up in India, he was deeply impressed to see how readily his missionary father responded to all the human needs around him. All the needs except one, that is.

Paul Brand tells of the day when he was seven years old and, for the first time, saw his father hesitate to help people in need. Three strangers arrived at the Brands' mountain home, each dressed in the breechcloth and turban common in that country. At first Paul thought they looked just like the hundreds of other people who came to the Brands for medical treatment. As he looked closer, however, he began to see differences. Their skin was mottled and they had thick, swollen foreheads and ears. Their feet were bandaged with bloodstained cloths, and they were missing both fingers and toes.

Paul Brand's mother, usually so hospitable, ordered both Paul and his sister inside the house and immediately sent for her husband. Paul sensed something strange going on, so instead of going inside, he quietly made his way to a place where he could watch. When his father arrived, he wore a pair of surgical gloves—unusual in that day—and seemed nervous around the strangers. Paul also noticed that, as his

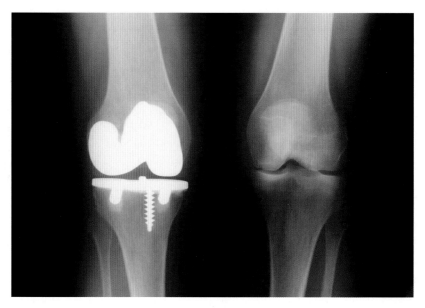

Research has led to new advances in treating damaged joints and bones.

Some Definitions

Respect: Showing high regard for other people. Treating others as you would want to be treated. Understanding that all people have value as human beings.

Compassion: Showing understanding of others by treating them with kindness, caring, generosity, and a forgiving spirit.

father washed and bandaged the men's sores, the men did not seem to be in any pain.

While Paul's father reluctantly cared for the visitors' sores, his mother set out fruit in a wicker basket for them. As the men left, they took the fruit but not the basket, and when little Paul went to retrieve it, his mother insisted he must not touch it. She wouldn't even let him go near the place where the men had sat. Paul watched his father burn the basket, then scrub his hands carefully. Paul and his sister then had to bathe, even though they had not been in any contact with the visitors.

That was Paul Brand's first view of leprosy, long considered one of the worst diseases known to humanity. Throughout history, leprosy victims have been shunned by other people and forced to stay in *sanitariums*. Some people suffering from leprosy could find no place else to go and so ended up in leper colonies, where they died slowly from the disease. Even though he knew all of this, Paul Brand eventually came to believe that his mission in life was to work with leprosy patients.

> **The Golden Rule**
>
> *Do unto others as you would have them do unto you.*
> This saying of Jesus Christ, recorded in the Christian New Testament, is considered to be the epitome of compassionate and respectful behavior.

Dr. Brand began his study of the disease in India. He spent years testing and observing patients, and at last proposed a theory that would change the world's understanding

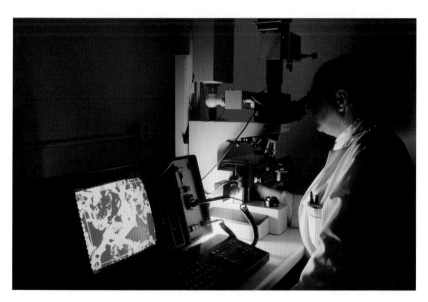

Research may require years of testing and observing.

of leprosy. Because so many patients were blind and missing fingers, toes, hands, and feet, the disease was believed to eat away at people's bodies. Paul Brand, however, did not believe leprosy was a flesh-devouring fungus. Instead, he proposed it was the loss of the sensation of pain that caused damage to the limbs. As people lost their ability to feel pain, they kept on using damaged body parts, and in the process damaged them further. (Think what would happen if you broke or sprained your foot but kept on using it so that it never had time to heal.) When leprosy patients lost the use of the nerve that makes the eyelid blink, their eyes dried out and they went blind. This loss of limbs and eyesight was obviously distressing to the patients with whom Dr. Brand worked, but beyond that, it diminished their ability to find employment and to care for themselves.

Brand and his team were committed to finding answers for one patient named Sadagopan, called Sadan by his friends. An educated and refined member of a high-caste Indian family, Sadan became an

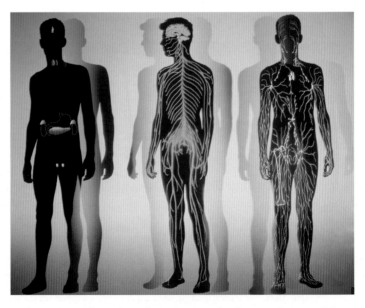

Research scientists have found answers and solutions for painful conditions that affect various human systems.

outcast because of his leprosy. People saw his sores and shrank from him. He could not eat in cafes, where they refused to serve him; buses would not allow him to ride. By the time Sadan went to Paul Brand's hospital in Vellore, India, his fingers were paralyzed and shortened, and his feet were covered with ulcerated sores and only half their normal length because of constant infection. Brand's team felt sure that Sadan's foot damage was due to his continuing to walk on already infected feet. They had him stay in bed until his feet healed, then began the long, arduous process of designing footwear which would allow him to walk without damaging his feet again. They tried every type of material available for various sandals and protective boots. Dr. Brand even went to Calcutta and England for training in using different kinds of plastics, hoping these might provide an answer. But time and time again, each shoe failed, and Sadan once again experienced infection.

Paul Brand was involved in his research with more than just his intellect; he felt deep respect and compassion for Sadan and the other patients with whom he worked. "More than a cold, scientific theory, the idea was almost like our own child. In the face of opposition from older, more experienced doctors . . . (we were) fighting for a cause that could conceivably overturn ancient prejudice against leprosy," he reported later in his book *Fearfully and Wonderfully Made.*

A PERSON OF CHARACTER . . .

treats others with respect . . .
is courteous and polite.
practices tolerance for others.
appreciates and accepts others.
does not abuse or mistreat others.
does not take advantage of
    others.
respects the rights and decisions
    of others.

shows caring and kindness . . .
demonstrates compassion to
    others.
follows the Golden Rule.
helps others.
refuses to be selfish, mean, or
    cruel to others.

Adapted from Character Counts Coalition, 4640 Admiralty Way, Suite 1001, Marina del Rey, California 90292.

The Hippocratic Oath

Medical doctors, whose practice is based on the research of scientists, are guided by four principles that can be traced back to Hippocrates (460?–377? BC), the man known as the "Father of Medicine." These four principles are:

1. Nonmaleficence—The physician was to "do no harm" to the patient, unless balanced by hope for improvement.
2. Beneficence—The physician would benefit the patient.
3. Autonomy—The patient is a self-determining agent and must give informed consent.
4. Justice—The principles of justice and equality must be followed.

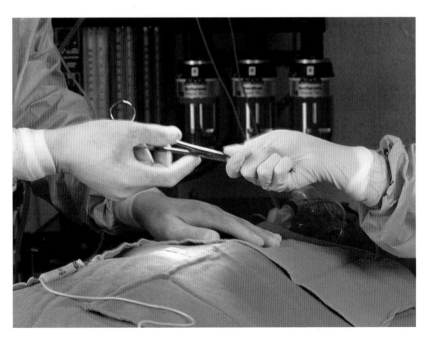

Like a medical doctor, a research scientist should "do no harm."

Five Questions to Ask Every Day

Dr. Paul Brand did his research out of deep respect and compassion, two character qualities he began learning as a child. Such qualities do not always develop naturally. Sometimes, we need tools to help us practice and become good at relating with character to other people. The following five questions, which we can ask ourselves every day, are such a tool:

1. Did I practice any virtues today?
   (Author William Bennett [*The Book of Virtues*] says that virtues are "habits of the heart" and that we learn them through models, usually grown-ups around us. Virtues include, but are not limited to, integrity, trustworthiness, honesty, and compassion. Virtues are the best parts of ourselves.)
2. Did I do more good than harm today?
   (To answer this, you must consider both short-term and long-term consequences.)
3. Did I treat people with dignity and respect today?
4. Was I fair and just today?
5. Was my community better because I was in it?
   ("Community" can be your neighborhood, family, company, church, etc.)

Material adapted from the Markkula Center for Applied Ethics.

Finally, after years of work, they developed a type of "rocker" boot that allowed Sadan's foot to rock rather than bend. Sadan eventually recovered enough to have a family and to proudly earn his living as a hospital record librarian. The "rocker" boot is now used in many areas of the world, not only for leprosy patients but for diabetics and other people who have insensitive feet.

Dr. Brand collected, organized, analyzed, and interpreted date, just as all research scientists do. He went one step further, though; he combined his scientific research with respect and compassion for others. Because he did, he made the world a better place.

The value of compassion cannot be over-emphasized. Anyone can criticize. It takes a true believer to be compassionate.

—Arthur H. Stainback

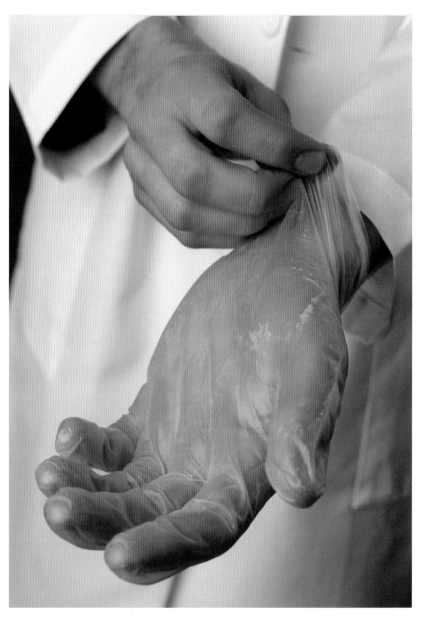

Researchers who work with the AIDS virus must be careful to protect themselves from infection.

4

JUSTICE AND FAIRNESS

The principles of justice and fairness
apply to the big things in life . . . as
well as the ordinary circumstances
we face every day.

When AIDS (Acquired Immune Deficiency Syndrome) first came to light in the early 1980s, research scientists around the world went to work to find a cause and a cure.

Luc Montagnier researched the AIDS problem in France, at the Pasteur Institute. Montagnier was born in 1932 and earned degrees in science and medicine at the Universities of Poitiers and Paris. He began working as a research scientist in 1955, joined the Pasteur Institute in 1972, and later became president of the Administrative Council of the European Federation for AIDS Research.

Meanwhile, Robert Gallo worked on the same issue at the National Cancer Institute in Bethesda, Maryland, in the United States. In 1984, Gallo announced that his research team had isolated the AIDS virus and that they had also developed a blood test to screen for the virus. Montagnier challenged Gallo's claim, pointing out the fact that he had previously sent Gallo samples of the virus isolated by French researchers.

The eyes of the scientific research world were fixed squarely on the controversy between these two men. At stake was the credit, and even glory, for being the first to isolate a virus that was spreading infection and fear around the globe. Isolating the virus was the first step in creating a screening test and, hopefully, developing a cure.

While Gallo's response to Montagnier's challenge was that the French specimens had not played a major role in the United States breakthrough, the French and American viruses were later found to be almost identical. HIV (human immunodeficiency virus) is a highly variable virus, depending on its source, and so the similarity of the viruses had to come from accidental or intentional use of the French virus by Gallo.

The bitter dispute seemed to be resolved in 1987 when the two research leaders agreed to share the credit. The United States government and the Pasteur Institute agreed to share the royalties from the blood test.

But the controversy wasn't over yet. In 1989 a *Chicago Tribune* reporter named John Crewdson wrote a long article about the dispute. This led to an investigation that supported Montagnier's claim to be

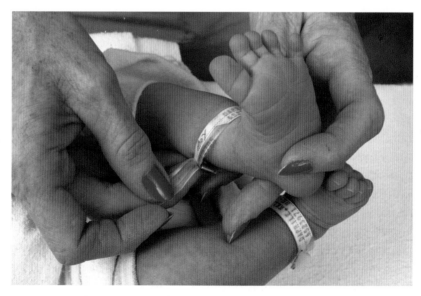

Each year, thousands of babies are born with AIDS.

Research teams may be funded by the government, by universities, or by other private organizations.

the first to isolate the HIV virus. Charges of misconduct were leveled at Gallo.

When research is funded by a government or a private organization, credit and financial gain are often important motivators. Conflict can boil up between competing research teams, causing bitter feelings between the parties and perhaps even slowing progress to a significant degree.

If this controversy had never taken up the time and energy and money of some of our greatest research scientists, might we be fur-

Justice is the end of government. It is the end of civil society. It ever has been, and ever will be pursued, until it be obtained, or until liberty be lost in the pursuit. In a society under the forms of which the stronger faction can readily unite and oppress the weaker, anarchy may as truly be said to reign, as in a state of nature where the weaker individual is not secured against the violence of the stronger. . . .
—James Madison

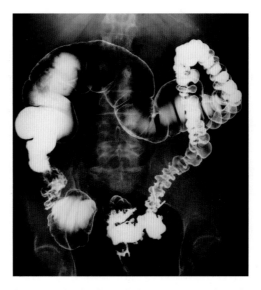

Because AIDS destroys the body's ability to resist other diseases, a person with AIDS may suffer from medical conditions that attack various body systems, including the digestive system.

ther along the road to a cure for AIDS–HIV? No one can answer with certainty, but it is a question worth consideration.

Fairness may be defined as practicing justice and equity, cooperating with one another, and recognizing the value of each individual. It is not always easy to be fair. Consider these situations:

- Your science class is divided into two-person teams for the annual state-wide science competition. Your team member—a boy who has few friends and is too shy to ever speak up in class—proposes an idea that would never have occurred to you. And his idea proves to be a winner. A month later, when the two of you are being congratulated by the governor in front of TV cameras for winning the entire state competition, you are the spokesperson. The governor shakes your hand and says, "One of the best science projects I've ever seen. Who came up with this idea?"

What do you say? Should you take credit as a team because you worked as a team? Should you point out that this was your partner's idea? You know that, even if you were to take credit for it, your partner would be far too shy to challenge you.

It is a natural human desire to be recognized for your work. Sometimes the recognition comes in the form of applause or awards. Sometimes it comes in money, or in higher esteem from others. When we face success, it can be difficult to share the recognition and rewards, even though others may deserve them as much as, or more than, we do.

Fairness says we need to value others as human beings who are equal in importance to ourselves. The Golden Rule (see chapter 3) teaches us to think of how we would like to be treated, then apply that treatment to others. It may be difficult to give credit to other classmates in school, but this is a situation that will come up again and again in the work place even when you are an adult. People of character are able to share recognition and credit with others who deserve it, and in practic-

Research scientists look for solutions to human beings' biggest problems—from disease to pollution.

A PERSON OF CHARACTER IS . . .

fair and just . . .

treats everyone fairly.

remains open-minded and listens to others.

does not take unfair advantage of others.

does not take more than their fair share.

Adapted from Character Counts Coalition, 4640 Admiralty Way, Suite 1001, Marina del Rey, California 90292.

ing this attitude of fairness, they can learn to work together for mutual benefit.

Aesop once told a story about a man who had several sons who could not work together in harmony but always argued among themselves. The father told his sons to bring him a bundle of sticks, and when they did, he told each son in turn to break this bundle over his knee. Each of his sons tried. Each of them failed.

Then the man took the sticks out of the bundle and gave his sons instructions to break them one by one, which they did easily. "Together," he told them, "you can stand unconquered against enemies. But when you quarrel and argue and try to stand alone, you can easily be conquered."

In science, as in so many other areas of life, justice and fairness contribute to teamwork and unity, important building blocks for cooperative research.

Questions of right and justice more or less underlie the commonest concerns of life.

—Alexander Crummell

In the modern world of science, being responsible takes time and thought.

5

RESPONSIBILITY

*Being responsible in today's world
takes careful thought.*

When England's King Richard III was preparing to fight at the Battle of Bosworth Field in 1485, his groom took the king's favorite horse to the blacksmith to be shod and ordered the blacksmith to hurry. The blacksmith quickly made the horseshoes and fastened on three of them. But he did not have enough nails to attach the fourth shoe properly.

When he told the groom that it would take time to make the necessary nails, the impatient groom couldn't wait. "Just use what you've got, can't you?" he said.

The blacksmith agreed, but he warned the groom that the fourth shoe wouldn't be as secure as the others.

When the Battle of Bosworth Field began, King Richard stayed right in the thick of the fighting, encouraging his men and urging them forward. Then he noticed some of his soldiers starting to retreat. Afraid that their example would influence the others, the king turned and galloped toward them in order to encourage them. Halfway across the field, however, one of his horse's shoes fell off. The horse stumbled and fell. Richard was thrown to the ground.

Terrified, the horse got up and galloped away. King Richard's soldiers turned and began running, and the enemy troops closed in around him.

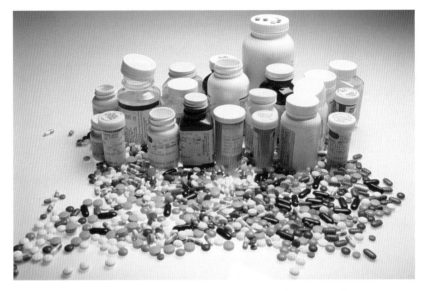

The many medicines on the market today are all the result of research scientists who did their jobs responsibly.

"A horse!" the king shouted. "My horse! My kingdom for a horse!"

But it was too late. His soldiers were running away. Soon the enemy got him, and the battle was over.

From this story came a poem about responsibility that people still quote:

> *For want of a nail, a shoe was lost,*
> *For want of a shoe, a horse was lost,*
> *For want of a horse, a battle was lost,*
> *For want of a battle, a kingdom was lost,*
> *And all for the want of a horseshoe nail.*

Sometimes, being responsible simply means working faithfully at the job that's assigned to you. Rachel Fuller Brown (1898–1980) was an American biochemist who did just that. Brown was born in Massachusetts, spent her childhood in Webster Groves, Missouri, and, when she was a teenager, returned to Massachusetts. She graduated from Mount Holyoke College in 1920 with a B.A. degree, having majored in history and chemistry. She later received her M.A. degree in organic chemistry and a Ph.D. in organic chemistry and bacteriology from the University of Chicago.

At first, Rachel Brown worked as an assistant chemist for the New York State Department of Health. She worked hard and met all her responsibilities, which resulted in promotions to positions requiring even more responsibility. In her 42 years at the Department of Health, she became first an assistant bio-

A PERSON OF CHARACTER . . .

acts responsibly . . .
is accountable to others.
considers the consequences for others before acting.
accepts responsibility for his or her choices.
does not blame others for his or her mistakes, or take credit for what others have done.
pursues excellence.
does not give up easily.
works hard to achieve.

Adapted from Character Counts Coalition, 4640 Admiralty Way, Suite 1001, Marina del Rey, California 90292.

In the Middle Ages, early scientists wanted to find a way to turn other materials into gold. Today, researchers may still be motivated by their greed for fame or fortune—or they may be responsible men and women who are seeking to help humanity.

chemist, then senior biochemist, associate biochemist, and finally, a research scientist.

Early in her career, Brown studied pneumococcus, the ***bacterium*** that causes pneumonia. She helped develop a pneumonia vaccine that is still used today. She went on to study fungi with a leading authority on the subject, Elizabeth Hazen. ***Microorganisms*** called actinomycetes live in the soil and produce antibiotics, but not all of these antibiotics are safe to use in human beings. Brown and Hazen worked to isolate these ***antifungal*** antibiotic substances from the soil, and test them for safety. When they isolated *Streptomyces norsei*, Brown discovered that it produced two antifungal substances, but one was too toxic for humans. The other substance was usable and was eventually named nystatin, named for the New York Department of Health Laboratories.

This drug is widely used today, marketed under the name Mycostatin, and it is prescribed for various yeast and fungal infections. It is also used to treat Dutch elm disease; to fight mold in the food industries, both for humans and livestock; and to kill mildew on fine artwork.

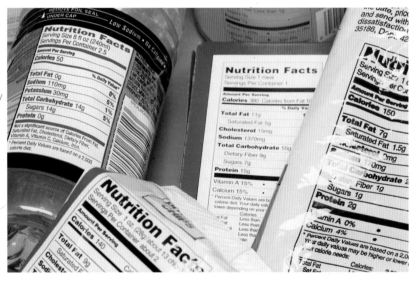

We owe our knowledge of nutrition and daily requirements to research scientists.

The word "respond" means to "answer." To be "responsible" means we are "answerable," or accountable.

Our first response when things go wrong is often "It wasn't me!" or "I didn't do it!" Our second response is often to blame others.

Conversely, our first response when things go right is often "It was me!" or "I did it!" and it can be difficult to give credit to others.

There is no end to the good you can do if you don't care who gets credit for it.
—Anonymous

Instead of accepting payment from royalties on nystatin, the two scientists used it to establish the Brown-Hazen Fund, which supports scientific research. Rachel Fuller Brown showed responsibility in her initial lower level job, which resulted in promotion to jobs where she was able to accomplish research of lasting benefit for the rest of the world.

At other times, being responsible means weighing the possible long-term effects, both good and bad, of our work. One issue currently forcing scientists to consider long-term effects is cloning. Scientists know of three ways to produce identical beings. The first way is very common and occurs often in nature, and is called "twinning" or "embryo cloning." Identical twins have not only identical nuclear DNA (all the same *genes*), but also identical ***mitochondrial*** DNA. Identical twins occur when the fertilized egg cell, or zygote, divides and forms two. The second method of making two genetically identical beings is nuclear transfer technology, in which the nucleus of a daughter cell of a fertilized egg cell is placed into an unfertilized egg cell of the same species. The third method is known as "true cloning," in which the adult animal's DNA is transferred to an unfertilized egg cell of the same species and the resulting animal is a genetically identical copy of the adult. This method was used to create Dolly the sheep and Cc the kitten.

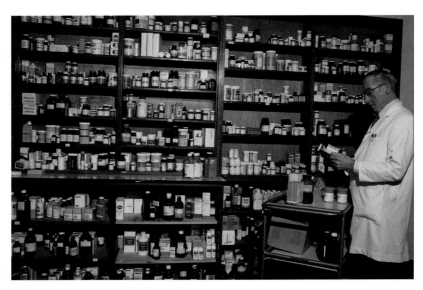

With new advances in medicine and pharmacology, come new responsibilities. Researchers need to be aware of the consequences of their work.

In the last few years, technology has moved forward so quickly that scientists now have the ability to do things that were impossible just a few years ago. Along with these abilities comes the responsibility to consider the consequences. Many people feel it does not automatically follow that, just because humans *can* do something, they *should* do it.

This rapid advancement of scientific knowledge, often termed the New Genetics, also includes stem cell research. Stem cell research has become a battleground for **ethicists**, some of whom praise the possibility of conquering certain devastating illnesses by use of stem cells. Others deplore the possibility that some scientists will clone new human embryos in order to harvest stem cells from them, which they consider creating and then destroying life in order to use it for self-serving ends.

Imagine these scenarios:

- Your cat, which you have owned and loved for over ten years, is hit by a car and killed. Would you take advantage of the new cloning technique that would allow you to have a kitten that is

In every cell nucleus of the body lies a strand of DNA, and each of these strands carries one hundred thousand genes which contain the instructions for what our cells should do. It has been estimated that our DNA has enough instructions to fill a thousand 600-page books. Even though all the DNA in one body could fit into an ice cube, if it were unwound and put together end to end, it could reach from the earth to the sun and back more than four hundred times.

an almost exact copy of your beloved cat? Would you consider the expense (at this writing estimated to be $30,000) to be justified? What if you were a parent who lost a child in a car accident and human cloning was possible?

- You are diagnosed with a fatal genetic disease. The doctors tell you that you will die within three to five years from this disease unless a new treatment, which in this case requires stem cells harvested from human embryos, is used. This new treatment could mean you will be able to live out your normal life span. You know that when the stem cells are harvested, the embryos have to die. The doctors say the choice is yours. What will you decide?
- Ethical questions are now being raised about scientific

Goals of the U.S. Human Genome Project

- Identify all the approximately 30,000 genes in human DNA.
- Determine the sequences of the 3 billion chemical base pairs that comprise human DNA.
- Store this information in databases.
- Improve tools for data analysis.
- Transfer related technologies to the private sector.
- Address the ethical, legal, and social issues that may arise from the project.

From the homepage of the Human Genome Project.

Questions from the Human Genome Project

The following questions are just a few from a long list of thought-provoking questions raised by the project:

- Who should have access to personal genetic information, and how will it be used?
- Who owns and controls genetic information?
- How does genomic information affect members of minority communities?
- What are the larger societal issues raised by new reproductive technologies?
- Who owns genes and other pieces of DNA?

From the homepage of the Human Genome Project.

techniques used to genetically modify plant life. Genetically modifying food can mean an increase in the food supply, an important consideration in a world where thousands starve to death every day. It can also mean that certain key nutrients can be delivered to people through their food supply, as in rice, which is modified to contain Vitamin A. Some people say genetically modified food can save and enhance life around the planet. Others caution that, as yet, we have no true idea of the dangers and negative consequences possible from altering our food supply in this way. If you lived in one of the underdeveloped countries of Asia where people frequently go blind for lack of Vitamin A, would you welcome or refuse the new "golden rice," which has been genetically altered to contain this vitamin and could help you and your family retain your eyesight?

- Genetically altered foods can contaminate the regular food supply by cross-pollination. Some countries insist that every food product containing genetically altered plants must be clearly marked. But some crops have been contaminated without anyone discovering it until the harvest reaches the consumer. How would you react if, as the owner of a large snack-food company, you lost huge amounts of money because your snack products were recalled from the market and discarded when genetically altered corn products were found to have contaminated your corn supply?

These hypothetical situations touch on the complexity of the decisions before research scientists now. The New Genetics seem to hold out great promise for the future, but there are significant questions that must be answered—and controls that must possibly be instituted—before many people will feel comfortable with the science involved.

Character is what you are in the dark.

—Dwight L. Moody

Researchers' work may seem like it would be the quiet sort that would not require much courage—but in reality, without courage, no one can practice any of the other character qualities.

6

COURAGE

*Courage is the character trait that
allows us to practice all the other
qualities of a good character.*

Jorge grew up in a large immigrant family in the southwestern United States. Their farm was small, and even though their few acres of irrigated vegetables required many hours of hard work from each family member, they never brought in much money. Jorge's parents had met in a migrant labor camp and married while they were still teenagers. Though they had not completed even a high school education, they cherished the dream that each of their seven children would not only graduate from high school, but from college as well.

As the oldest child in the family, much of the responsibility for the family's vegetable crops fell upon Jorge's shoulders. His favorite activity, though, was to visit the ranch next door. The ranch was owned by a veterinarian, Dr. Stevenson, who raised horses and beef cattle, along with a few chickens. Jorge spent every hour he could steal away from his responsibilities at the neighboring ranch. He tagged along behind Dr. Stevenson and dreamed of the day when he, too, could have cattle and chickens and—the most beautiful of all—horses.

As Jorge grew older, he began to help the veterinarian with some of his farm tasks. He asked hundreds of questions about animal care, and

Dr. Stevenson loaned him books and journals on the subject. By the time Jorge was in high school, he knew exactly what he wanted to do with his life—study medicine and research new ways to treat and cure the diseases of the animals he loved so much. But how could someone like him, with no money at all, ever afford the years of medical training involved?

At the end of Jorge's junior year of high school, Dr. Stevenson told him about a scholarship funded by the medical association to which he belonged. "I've been watching you for years, Jorge, and I know how much you want to work with animals," the doctor told him. "Helping you study medicine will benefit all of us in the end."

To Jorge, the scholarship seemed like a miracle. His parents were amazed. Their first child would not only be able to attend college but to go on to veterinary school and then to a respected, well-paying career. It seemed their dream was coming true.

Jorge's years at a nearby university were all he could have hoped

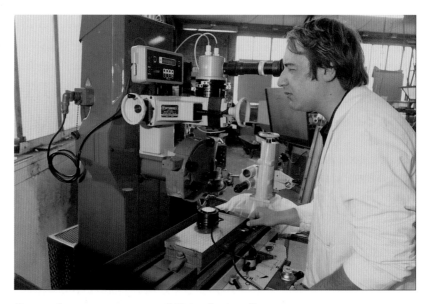

Researchers open new possibilities for us all.

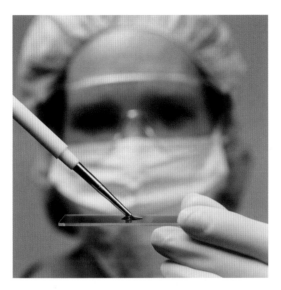

People who value courage do the right thing—in big ways that draw lots of attention, and in small, quiet ways that no one may ever notice.

for. He was an excellent student and enjoyed the affirmation of his professors during both his undergraduate and graduate studies. Best of all, he spent long hours in the laboratory because one of his professors, the head of the scholarship committee, had invited him to participate in a major research project. The project was an exciting one, working on a new drug that promised help for many animals.

After many months of observation and analysis, however, Jorge noticed that, no matter what he did, he could not duplicate some of the results his professor claimed to have achieved. He checked and rechecked his work, going over and over each calculation painstakingly. When he spoke to the professor about

People who value courage:

- say what's right (even when no one agrees with them).
- do the right thing (even when it's hard).
- follow their conscience (instead of the crowd).

Collecting accurate data is essential to good research.

this problem, he noticed that the older man seemed defensive. Soon their relationship began to cool, and Jorge found himself feeling increasingly alone in his research.

As Jorge checked his professor's work more and more closely, he realized with a sick feeling in the pit of his stomach that he must be looking at data that had been purposely changed to support a previous conclusion. Jorge knew he must begin writing his dissertation soon, but the very foundation of all his research was now in serious question.

He tried again to speak to his professor about the problem, but got nowhere. Then Jorge explained that, under the circumstances, he had no choice but to go to the department chair and explain the situation. At this, the professor exploded in anger and ordered Jorge out of his office, adding that if Jorge said a word about this to anyone, he would lose his scholarship faster than he could imagine.

Jorge was so frightened by the professor's threat that he was unable to decide what to do. How could he voluntarily step forward, knowing

A Framework for Ethical Decision Making

1. Recognize a moral issue.
   * Ask yourself if there is something wrong, either personally or socially.
   * Are there conflicts in place that could damage people, animals, institutions or society?
   * Go beyond concerns about legality. Does this issue affect the dignity and rights of individuals?
2. Get the facts.
   * Investigate the relevant facts.
   * Decide which people have a stake in the outcome of this issue, and what that stake is.
   * Determine your options for acting.
   * Get the opinion of someone you respect.
   * Make sure you have consulted all persons and groups involved.
3. Evaluate options from different moral perspectives.
   * Which option will do the most good, while doing the most harm?
   * Which option respects the rights and dignity of all stakeholders?
   * Will each be treated fairly?
   * Which option best promotes the common good?
   * Which option encourages the development of the virtues and character traits that we value?
4. Make a decision.
   * Considering all the questions above, which of the options is the right one?
   * Get the opinion of someone you respect on the option you've chosen.
5. Reflect afterward.
   * Look back and determine how your decision turned out for everyone involved.
   * Would you choose the same option if you had it to do over again?

Material adapted from the Markkula Center for Applied Ethics.

he could lose his scholarship and his chance to fulfill his life-long dream? And what about his parents, who had quietly, faithfully labored in the fields all their adult lives just so Jorge could have this opportunity?

But how could he live with himself if he kept silent?

Jorge decided to sit down with a pen and paper in hand and follow the Framework for Ethical Decision Making that had been presented in one of his classes, writing out each step to get it clear in his mind.

1. Recognize a Moral Issue

Jorge knew that this was a moral and ethical issue known to scientists as falsification, which means misreporting or actually changing data or results. If the study went forward based on incorrect data, it could eventually lead to many animals being harmed and even facing death. It was also a matter of violating the trust of veterinarians and animal owners.

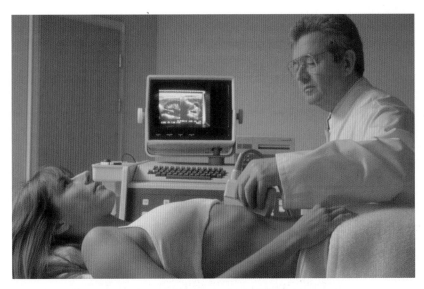

The research performed on animals often leads to new advances in human medicine as well.

2. Get the Facts

Jorge had done all he could possibly do to verify his facts and conclusions. The obvious people with a stake in this matter were himself and the professor. Beyond that, however, animal owners, veterinarians, and the pharmaceutical company that hoped to produce the new drug all had a stake in this. So did the university itself. Tainted research would eventually affect them all.

As Jorge tried to determine his options for acting, he knew he could keep silent. He wouldn't have to actually falsify anything in his dissertation if he simply used his professor's data as an accepted starting point.

Or he could follow the ethics guidelines of the university research center and his own conscience, and go to the department chair. A committee would be convened to look into the issue and decide what should happen next.

Jorge wondered if he had other options he couldn't see. He picked up the phone and asked Dr. Stevenson's advice.

3. Evaluate Options from Different Moral Perspectives

After his conversations with his mentor, Jorge felt clearer about his choices. When he tried to evaluate the option of staying silent, he knew it could result in what looked like immediate good. He would retain his scholarship and keep the short-term good will of the faculty. But when the facts were found out, perhaps years down the road, what then? The situation would be made worse by the fact that he had participated in a cover-up.

On the other hand, his choice to tell the facts to the department chair would certainly result in what appeared to be serious harm. If an investigating committee found Jorge's facts correct, his professor's reputation would be seriously damaged, if not destroyed. At the same time, however, many other people and animals, would be spared harm. There was a chance that the professor could make his threat about the scholarship stick. But once the facts were on the table, Jorge hoped other committee members might come to his aid. Either way, Jorge knew that this option was in keeping with his own personal morals and the qualities he wanted to be part of his character.

4. Make a Decision

Jorge put down his pen and looked up from the sheet of notebook paper he had filled. He knew now what he had to do, even if the situation turned out badly for him. Still, this was too big a matter to decide alone. Jorge knew he needed the opinion of someone neutral, someone he could trust. He picked up the phone and again called Dr. Stevenson to see if he was free that evening.

After talking things over with Dr. Stevenson, what do you think Jorge decided to do? What would you do in his place?

Everything that's worthwhile in life is scary. Choosing a school, choosing a career, getting married, having kids—all those things are scary. If it is not fearful, it is not worthwhile.

—*Paul Tournier*

In the 18th century, researchers began to study the world around them. Their work led to a scientific revolution.

7

SELF-DISCIPLINE AND DILIGENCE

Success doesn't happen by accident—it takes hard work.

Although it is now common knowledge that insects are responsible for pollinating many different kinds of flowers, no one knew this information until a German naturalist named Christian Konrad Sprengel (1750–1816) began studying them. At first Christian Sprengel, whose job was teaching, studied plants only in his spare time. But as he became more and more interested in plants, he decided to devote his life to studying them. Through years of observing plants carefully and diligently, he eventually discovered that the special colors of different flowers are designed to attract various insects, which are responsible for carrying grains of pollen from the stamen to the pistil.

As Sprengel continued to observe plants, he saw that stamens and pistils mature at different times in some flowers. He learned that flowers cannot pollinate themselves but must be pollinated by other flowers of the same kind. Sprengel's diligent observations were eventually printed in his book, *The Newly Revealed Mystery of Nature in the Structure and Fertilization of Flowers*, and although his work was ignored for many years, its importance was eventually recognized by other scientists.

Not everyone who does valuable research is a trained scientist. Sometimes, people are so interested in the world around them that they

Computer technology allows researchers new ways to explore the world.

put tremendous energy into learning about it. One such person, Wilson A. Bentley (1865–1931), grew up in Jericho, Vermont, on a dairy farm. Though Wilson had no special scientific training, he was so fascinated by snowflakes that he taught himself to photograph them through a microscope, a difficult and painstaking process. Over the course of his lifetime, Wilson took well over five thousand of these photomicrographs and published 2,500 of them in a book called *Snow Crystals* in 1931. His work proved that no two snowflakes are alike.

Other people do research to help someone they love, and through self-discipline and diligence, they research until they make great discoveries. Lorenzo Odone's parents were two such people.

When Lorenzo Odone was five, he suddenly began having problems

---

Some Definitions

Self-discipline: regulation of oneself for the sake of improvement.
Diligence: steady, earnest, energetic effort.

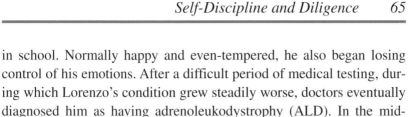

in school. Normally happy and even-tempered, he also began losing control of his emotions. After a difficult period of medical testing, during which Lorenzo's condition grew steadily worse, doctors eventually diagnosed him as having adrenoleukodystrophy (ALD). In the mid-1980s, when Lorenzo was diagnosed, there was no treatment for this disease. ALD meant certain death, usually within two years of diagnosis.

However, Lorenzo's parents, Augusto and Michaela Odone, were determined to do everything they could to save their son. Doctors, scientists, and even the support groups for parents of other children with ALD discouraged the Odones from trying. No one believed the Odones could find an answer to this terrible disease, not when many highly trained research scientists had already failed to do so.

But the Odones refused to give up. They used the scientific method to investigate ALD, and they built models of the very long chain of unsaturated fatty acids involved in adrenoleukodystrophy. They traveled to libraries and read everything they could find on the subject, and they

Earliest research scientists began by studying the heavens. Based on their work, new methods of observation were shaped—and these eventually led to the scientific methods researchers still follow today

Research Yourself!

Wilson Bentley knew what interested him. So did Christian Konrad Sprengel. For both of these men, their interests led to their life's work. Do you know what kinds of things interest you? Here's a simple way to begin finding out.
   Ask yourself:

• What is my favorite subject in school?
• What kinds of books do I best like to read? (Fiction? Biography? History?)
• If I could choose any television programs I wanted to watch (aside from sitcoms), what kinds of programs would they be? (Nature programs? Travelogues? Mysteries?)
• If I could go anywhere I wanted on vacation, where would it be? (Seashore? Mountains? Desert? Islands?)
• What do I wonder about most in the world around me?

Answering these questions can help you discover your unique interests, and maybe give you ideas as to what you might some day like to research.

talked to people around the world who had information on ALD. And all the while, they had to keep on caring for Lorenzo, whose condition grew worse and worse.

Sometimes Augusto and Michaela were so exhausted they felt they couldn't go on for another day; sometimes they felt that their marriage might be falling apart under all the stress. But they kept on working until they discovered that a mixture of oleic acid and uric acid, which they called Lorenzo's Oil, could help prevent, or at least greatly reduce, the symptoms of ALD. Today, many children who would have died from ALD just a few decades ago can take Lorenzo's Oil and live healthy, symptom-free lives because of the Odone's research and discovery.

One symptom of ALD is the breakdown of myelin, a substance that

A century ago, the life span was far shorter than it is today. We owe our extended lives to the discoveries of research scientists.

coats the nerves and is necessary for our nervous system to work properly. Demyelination of cells (stripping away the myelin) can eventually lead to blindness, hearing loss, paralysis, dementia, and the inability to speak. Lorenzo's Oil, which can prevent further demyelination, cannot replace the myelin that has been destroyed by ALD. The Odones found that research scientists around the world working on myelin regeneration needed a way to cooperate and share information, so they set up

CHARACTER . . .

is what you do, not what you say.
is made up of your choices.
requires doing the right thing, even if it costs you.
is a standard you choose for yourself, not a standard modeled on the bad behavior of others.
has a payoff—it makes you a better person and the world a better place.
can make a difference, even if you stand alone.

the Myelin Project, which funds research and brings researchers together. The project has made significant progress and scientists feel that remyelination of the human nervous system may be possible in the very near future. The Odones' self-discipline and diligence in researching ALD continues to help many people.

Let me tell the secret that has led to my goal. My strength lies solely in my tenacity.

—Louis Pasteur, research scientist who
discovered a vaccine against polio

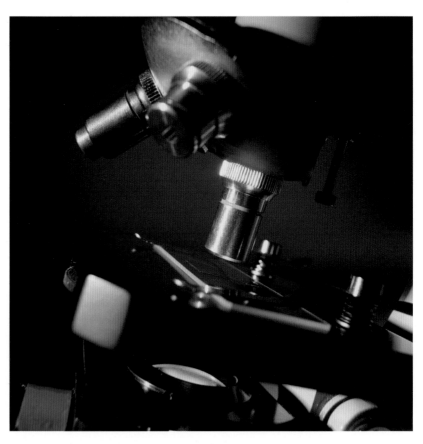

Some scientists may study the far reaches of space with enormous telescopes—while other researchers focus on the tiny world inside the cell.

8

CITIZENSHIP

Being a good citizen often depends on the choices we make.

Good citizens do their share to make their world better. Research scientists do this by cooperating with one another and by working not only for their own good, but for the good of the community. When scientists see people suffering from a disease and decide to research a cure, they are displaying good citizenship and working to make their world a better place.

When Canadian molecular geneticist and Nobel prize winner Lap-Chee Tsui (pronounced "Choy") saw that cystic fibrosis kills about one out of every 2,000 of his fellow Canadians (mostly children), he decided to research the cause and possible cure for this disease. Cystic fibrosis (CF) is the most common disease among white people and is caused by a genetic *mutation*, which causes the mucous in the lungs, nose, and mouth to be so thick that breathing is difficult. Half of the children born with CF will die before they are 25; few live beyond 30.

Using microbiological techniques, Tsui first had to localize the CF gene to a particular region of chromosome 7, which has 150,000,000 base pairs or units of DNA. The region where the CF gene is found has 230,000 DNA base pairs which spell out a series of 1,480 amino acids that make up the Cystic Fibrosis Transmembrane Conductance Regulator (CFTR) protein. Just one missing amino acid here causes the majority of cases of CF.

May 9, 1989 was the day that Tsui and his colleagues discovered the gene for CF, but even after that exciting day, they spent five months doing their tests over and over to see whether their results would be the same, making sure their discovery was real. Since then, Tsui's team has gone on to correct the CF defect in a dish in the laboratory by inserting normal genes into cells from CF patients. Correcting the defect in actual patients, however, has not worked yet. But Tsui's discovery has made it possible to research CF in animals, bringing the possibility of therapy

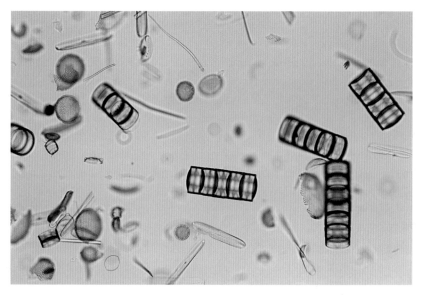

The microscope reveals a hidden world we would never suspect.

Researchers' work builds a better community for us all.

and even a cure much closer. Also, it is now possible to diagnose CF in the unborn, and even to test couples before they become pregnant, to see if they are CF carriers. Lap-Chee Tsui and the team of researchers who worked with him have expressed their citizenship by making an important contribution to their community, nation, and world, one which holds out the promise of making life better for thousands of people.

Citizenship is not confined only to making positive discoveries. Our choices about how we use

Citizenship can mean . . .

- volunteering to pick up the trash in your local park.
- obeying your community's laws (on curfew, loitering, handicapped parking, etc.).
- *staying informed so that you can vote as soon as you are old enough.*
- helping a neighbor shovel snow or rake leaves.
- showing respect for people in authority like policemen and teachers.

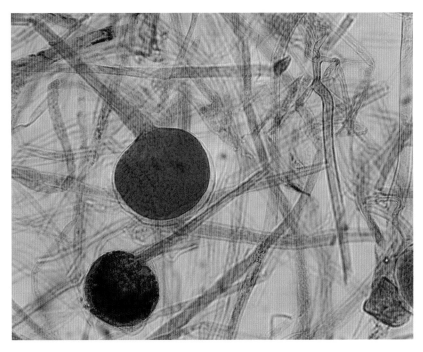

The knowledge gained from researchers' study of microscopic cells helps create longer and better lives for the entire living community.

Character

Your character is defined by what you do, not what you say or believe.

Your choices define the kind of person you are choosing to be.

Good character means doing what's right, even when it costs you something.

One person can make a difference. What *you* do matters.

Practicing good character qualities makes you a better person and the world a better place.

Adapted from goodcharacter.com.

medical discoveries already made, and about the use or non-use of certain medical techniques and drugs can also mark us as people whose behavior is governed by the principles of good citizenship. Sometimes we must choose between obeying laws enacted for the welfare of the community and obeying our own desire to help a friend. Consider these situations:

- You have a friend who is in great pain because of a ***chronic*** disease. She asks you to buy marijuana for her. You know that marijuana, used medicinally, offers pain relief, and you want very much to help this friend. However, marijuana use—medicinal or not—is illegal where you live. Fulfilling your friend's request would mean breaking the law. Another concern you have is how your friend would parent her two toddlers while under the influence of this drug, and you feel you have an obligation to see that these children are protected. What would you do?

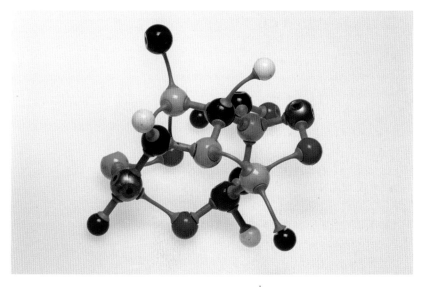

Researchers gain understanding of our world by studying the chemical construction of various substances.

- You and your spouse go through genetic testing prior to conceiving your first child. You learn that you have a fifty-fifty chance of bearing a child with cystic fibrosis. You understand that most CF children die before age 25, and only a few live to see 30. Will you take the chance? Or will you decide to adopt— or remain childless?

You may never face decisions this difficult. But we all must make decisions about the kind of citizens we will be.

A nation, as a society, forms a moral person, and every member of it is personally responsible for his society.

—Thomas Jefferson

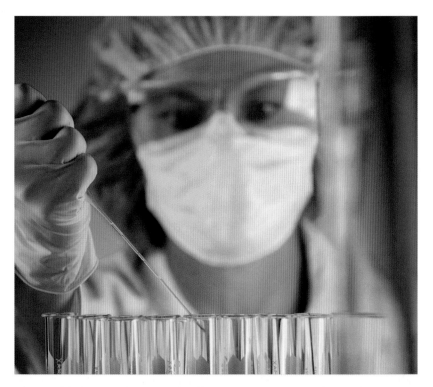

The world of scientific research offers opportunities for those who are curious about their world.

9

CAREER OPPORTUNITIES

*Human beings have always been—and will
always be—curious about the world around
them and the world inside their own bodies.
As long as this curiosity remains, research
scientists will be in demand.*

Annelise Barron is an assistant professor at Northwestern University. She's also a chemical engineer—and a researcher. She is a research team leader for her team of graduate and postdoctoral students who are experimenting with Barron's idea that synthetic molecules might be used as a drug to help doctors treat a variety of lung ailments, specifically those of premature infants.

Annelise wears many hats, and in doing so, she typifies today's research scientist. She must oversee the many projects going on in her lab, and still prepare lectures and fulfill all the duties of a teacher. Recently married and now expecting her first child, Annelise speaks wistfully of a day when she will not be working at such a frenetic pace. Still, her dedication is obvious. She's convinced that the synthetic molecules her lab is trying to produce may give premature infants a better chance at life, and nothing stands in her way of pursuing that dream.

Annelise is like many of the thousands of research scientists who work diligently, often in several capacities, to fulfill their dream

Earnings

In 1998, median annual earnings for biological scientists were $46,140. Those employed by the Federal Government earned $48,600; in drug companies, $46,300; in research and testing services, $40,800; and in State Government (except education and hospitals), $38,000.

In 1998, median annual earnings for medical scientists were $50,410.

In 1999, the National Association of Colleges and Employers reported beginning salary offers averaged $29,000 for those with bachelor's degrees in biological science; $34,450 for those with master's degrees, and $45,700 for those with doctoral degrees.

In 1999, federal government general biological scientists in nonsupervisory and supervisory positions averaged $56,000; microbiologists $62,600; ecologists, $57,100; physiologists, $71,300; and geneticists, $68,200.

Material adapted from U.S. Department of Labor *Occupational Outlook Handbook, 2000–2001.*

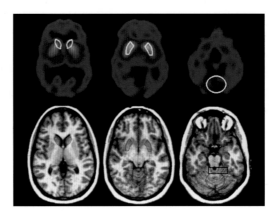

With constantly advancing technology, research scientists have ever-new opportunities to explore the universe . . . the earth . . . and the human body.

*Research scientists face considerable competition in university-
funded labs.*

of discovering a way to combat certain diseases, to save the environment for future generations, and to help their fellow human
beings.

Outlook for Ph.D.s

Biological and medical scientists face considerable competition for in-
dependent research positions. Because the federal government funds so
much of basic research and development, government budget tighten-
ing leads to limiting both the numbers of grants given and the dollar
amount of grants. As more and more advanced degrees in this field are
awarded, competition levels may continue to increase. Another con-
tributing factor is the highly competitive job market for college and university faculty, which leads more scientists to seek jobs in private industry than was the case in the past.

The work of research scientists touches the lives of all of us. These researchers all changed our world.

Nikolai Basov won a Nobel Prize for helping to develop the maser, an intense beam of microwave radiation that later laid the foundation for lasers.

Rosa Beddington discovered how an embryo forms during its earliest stages.

Ugo Fano played an important role in the early development of modern atomic physics and carried out the first controlled nuclear chain reaction.

William Federspiel invented a temporary artificial lung.

Viktor Hamburger charted the structure of the human embryo's developing nervous system.

Ariel Loewy learned how blood clots form by identifying factor XIII, the enzyme that binds proteins together to create a plug in a wound.

Natalie Mandzhavidze investigated solar flares, which affect power transmission systems on Earth.

John O'Brien discovered the genetic cause of Tay-Sachs disease.

John Rust identified cancer in cattle exposed to the U.S. testing of the first atomic bomb and warned the world of the dangers of radiation.

Leslie Thompson discovered a potential way to treat Huntington's disease.

Outlook for Bachelor's or Master's Degrees

Opportunities are expected to be better at this level. Non-Ph.D.s, who usually qualify for jobs in sales, marketing, and research management, should find such positions more plentiful. They may also take positions as science or health technicians, or become high school biology teachers. In the last decade of the 20th century, biotechnology companies increased rapidly, requiring many new staff members. This growth is expected to slow as such firms merge or are absorbed into larger ones.

Expansion is expected in research on gene therapies, AIDS, cancer, and Alzheimer's disease. Scientists in the biological and medical fields are less likely to lose their jobs during recessions because they are often working on long-term research projects.

Throughout human history, people whose curiosity has motivated them to observe and study the world around them have been responsible for advances that have made life better, safer, and more comfortable for the rest of us. These researchers have combined their desire to know

Today's research scientists need an understanding of computer technology.

more about their world with diligence and courage, with responsibility and compassion and integrity, and have made the world a better place for us to live together. Without research scientists, we would have no antibiotics to combat bacterial infections. Children around the world would still live in dread of being paralyzed by polio, and there would be no help for leprosy patients and those afflicted by hundreds of other diseases.

Research scientists are people who face problems squarely and say, "I think I can learn more about how to solve this." And when they combine their technical and scientific knowledge with strong character qualities, they can make great and lasting contributions to the human race.

Try not to become a [person] of success, but rather a [person] of value.

—Albert Einstein

Further Reading

Bennett, William J. *The Book of Virtues for Young People.* New York: Simon & Schuster for Young Readers, 1997.

Brand, Paul and Philip Yancey. *Fearfully and Wonderfully Made.* Grand Rapids, Mich.: Zondervan, 1980.

Hopke, William E., editor. *The Encyclopedia of Careers and Vocational Guidance*, Ninth Edition. Chicago: J. G. Ferguson Publishing Company, 1993.

Josephson, Michael S. and Wes Hanson, editors. *The Power of Character.* San Francisco: Jossey-Bass, 1998.

Kidder, Rushworth M. *How Good People Make Tough Choices.* New York: Simon & Schuster, 1995.

The U.S. Department of Labor. *Occupational Outlook Handbook, 2001.* Washington, D.C.: U.S. Government Printing Office, 2001.

FOR MORE INFORMATION

American Institute of Biological Sciences
Suite 200
1444 I Street NW
Washington, D.C. 20005
www.aibs.org

The Best Source for Canadian Science
www.science.ca

Bio-Rad
Corporate Human Resource
1000 Alfred Nobel Dr.
Hercules, California 94547
www.bio-rad.com/

The Biotechnology Industry Organization (BIO)
1625 K Street, N.W.
Suite 1100
Washington, D.C. 20006-1604

Character Education Network
www.charactered.net

Genentech, Inc.
Human Resources
Dept. XRC
460 Point San Bruno Blvd.
South San Francisco, California 94080
www.gene.com/

Howard Hughes Medical Institute
www.hhmi.org

Josephson Institute of Ethics
www.josephsoninstitute.org

Information on Careers in Biology, Conservation, and Oceanography
www.si.edu/resource/faq/nmnh/careers.htm

GLOSSARY

Antibiotics   Substances that can kill microorganisms like bacteria.

Antifungal   Possessing the ability to kill fungi.

Bacterium   A one-celled microorganism that can cause infection or disease; the plural is "bacteria."

Chemotherapy   Treating or controlling a disease or mental illness by means of a chemical agent.

Chronic   A disease marked by long duration or frequent recurrence.

Clinical trials   Testing a new medicine in studies where the results can be closely observed and recorded.

Cloning   The process of producing a genetically identical group of cells from a single ancestor.

Codified   Reduced to a code or system.

DNA   Deoxyribonucleic acid, molecules that are long chains of instructions for making proteins.

Ethicist   A specialist in the study of good and bad and the principles of conduct governing an individual or group.

Genes   Material that carries information for making all the proteins required by all organisms. These proteins determine how the organism looks and carries on basic functions, such as metabolizing food or fighting infection.

Genome   All the DNA in an organism, including its genes.

Human Genome Project   A large project to map and sequence all DNA in human chromosomes.

Mitochondrial   Having to do with the part of the cell that produces energy.

Mutation   A significant and basic alteration.

Oncologist   A doctor who specializes in treating cancer.

Sanitariums   Institutions that provided treatment (or at least a place to rest) for people who were chronically ill.

INDEX

applied research 7

bacteria 5, 6
Basov, Nicolai 82
Beddington, Rosa 82
Bentley, Wilson A. 64, 66
biological research 7, 10
biological scientists 7, 8, 10, 11, 81, 83
biological technologists 10
biologists, types 11
biology teachers 10, 81
biotechnology companies 83
Brand, Paul 25–29, 31, 32
breakthrough discoveries 19
Brown, Rachel Fuller 44–47

character 1–3, 20, 21, 29, 40, 45, 51, 53, 60,
    67, 72, 74, 84
clinical trials 8
clinics 8
cloning 9, 12, 47, 48
communication 12
computers 10
contamination 8
core character qualities 12, 31

data 6, 10, 19, 56, 58, 59
deception in science 18, 35–37, 55–56, 58–60
degree requirements 10–11
DNA 8, 47, 49, 50, 71
drug industry 8
drug therapy 11

earnings 82
earth research 7
educational institutions 8, 10
environmental research 7
ethical decisions 12, 19, 49, 57
ethicists 48

Fano, Ugo 82
Federspiel, William 82
Fleming, Sir Alexander 5, 6

Gallo, Robert 35, 36, 37
genes 47, 49, 50, 71, 72, 83
gene therapy 11
genome 9
Golden Rule, The 27, 29, 39
government jobs 8
grants 8, 81

Hamburger, Viktor 82
Hazen, Elizabeth 46
Hippocratic Oath, The 30
hospitals 8
Human Genome Project, The 9, 49, 50

laboratories 8, 9, 10
laboratory animals 8
Loewy, Ariel 83
Lorenzo's Oil 66

Mandzhavidze, Natalie 82
medical laboratory technologists 10
medical research 7
medical scientists 7, 8, 11, 12, 81, 83
Montagnier, Luc 35, 36
mutation 71
Myelin Project, The 67

National Institutes of Health 8, 9
New Genetics 48, 51
nuclear transfer technology 47

O'Brien, John 82

Pasteur, Louis 69
private industry 7, 81
product development 7, 10

research assistants 10
research and development 7, 81
research institutes 19
research scientists 12, 19, 35, 46
research teams 7, 37, 79
Rust, John 83

safety procedures 8
Salk, Jonas Edward 6
sanitariums 27
scientific method 17, 65
social sciences 7
Sprengel, Christian Konrad 63, 66
statistical analysis 10
stem cell research 48

Thompson, Leslie 82
Tsui, Lap Chi 5, 71, 72

virtues 31

Watson and Crick 8

BIOGRAPHIES

Shirley Brinkerhoff is a writer, editor, speaker, and musician. She graduated Summa Cum Laude from Cornerstone University with a Bachelor of Music degree, and from Western Michigan University with a Master of Music degree. She has published six young adult novels, scores of short stories and articles, and teaches at writers' conferences throughout the United States.

Cheryl Gholar is a Community and Economic Development Educator with the University of Illinois Extension. She has a Ph.D. in Educational Leadership and Policy Studies from Loyola University, and she has more than 20 years of experience with the Chicago Public Schools as a teacher, counselor, guidance coordinator, and administrator. Recognized for her expertise in the field of character education, Dr. Gholar assisted in developing the K–12 Character Education Curriculum for the Chicago Public Schools, and she is a five-year participant in the White House Conference on Character Building for a Democratic and Civil Society. The recipient of numerous awards, she is also the author of *Beyond Rhetoric and Rainbows: A Journey to the Place Where Learning Lives.*

Ernestine G. Riggs is an Assistant Professor at Loyola University Chicago and a Senior Program Consultant for the North Central Regional Educational Laboratory. She has a Ph.D. in Educational Leadership and Policy Studies from Loyola University, and she has been involved in the field of education for more than 35 years. An advocate of teaching the whole child, she is a frequent presenter at district and national conferences; she also serves as a consultant for several state boards of education. Dr. Riggs has received many citations, including an award from the United States Department of Defense Overseas Schools for Outstanding Elementary Teacher of America.